RedeemHer
Heart

RedeemHer Heart

the stories we hide behind

JENNIFER WRIGHT

RedeemHer Heart
the stories we hide behind

© 2020 RedeemHer Heart

COVER & TEXT DESIGN BY Jazmin Welch
COVER IMAGE BY Goran Ivos via Unsplash
BACK COVER IMAGE BY Bee Balogun via Unsplash
FAMILY PHOTO & HEADSHOT BY Venetia Gault of Salt and Sparrow
EDITED BY The Studio Press
PUBLISHING ASSISTANCE The Studio Press

All rights reserved.

No part of this publication may be reproduced, stored in a retrieval system or transmitted in any form or by any means—electronic, mechanical, photocopying or otherwise—without the prior written consent of the author.

ISBN 978-1-7771734-1-8

To my first love and superhero—My Dad! Miss you every day, thank you for the legacy you left behind, and especially for cultivating in me—the tenacious spirit to never give up and to have no fear!

For my Zion Angel girl, loving you forever. Too beautiful for this earth.

To my beautiful grandparents—Sealitu, Tuavalu, Samoa and Amosa, missing your wisdom, your stories and your warm love

To my spiritual mentor and dearest friend—Elwyn Scale, your influence, character and guidance changed my faith forever, the imprint you left on my heart is huge, I have forever gratitude to you and your ministry of breaking chains and restoring lives, you were a gifted visionary, so far ahead of our time, absolute legend! Rest in Love.

I am so looking forward to seeing you all again on that glorious resurrection morning!

Love Jen xx

contents

the intention · 9

fighting · 11

something to prove · 17

perfection has its price · 23

too beautiful for this earth · 31

season of loss · 37

falling short · 53

the search · 69

denying myself · 79

fought 93

the intention

I'VE ASKED MYSELF THROUGHOUT this whole process; why am I writing this book? Why would I want to share the deepest, darkest, and most vulnerable moments of my life with the world? *Who would want to know about what I went through? Why does my story matter?*

As I reflect on the intention behind this book you're about to read, I've come to realize that my story is not about me, it's about you. You are my intention and the heart of my book.

Through all that life throws at you that is completely out of your control, know that weeping may endure for the night, but joy comes in the morning.

RedeemHer Heart is my journey towards taking back my power from the seasons of constant fighting, striving, and surviving. It is closing a chapter of my life when I was living out of alignment with who God created me to be. The time when I was focused on living out distorted beliefs, pleasing people, constantly searching for answers, and the next best thing and just not being who I am. Redemption looks different for everyone, but for me, it has been a deliverance from the strongholds of mistruths, trauma, and hiding in shame.

These are my real-life events. These are raw thoughts and conversations with myself, hence the conversational style of this book. I view my experiences as different chapters, or as I like to call them, seasons. This is not a "how-to" book with a solution-based framework, but rather an opportunity for you to take what your heart needs or desires in this season of your life.

From my heart to yours,
Jen xx

1

fighting

I CAME INTO THIS WORLD FIGHTING, and I'll go out the same way.

A few hours after I was born, my mum felt like something wasn't right. As it turns out, I had pneumonia.

As a little girl, I would read our family bible heirloom because my mother had penned the experience of my birth. In it, she wrote how I was taken to the ICU, and the outlook was very grim. In the 24 hours following my birth, there was a collective of prayer and fasting being uplifted on my behalf. Since you're reading this, you know I survived. The doctors said, "this one is a fighter."

I was quite a sick child. My mum would tell me of providential incidences where she was sure I could have died. There was a time we were at church, and I had fallen asleep, so she laid me in the back seat of our Ford Falcon. She went back into the church but began to feel that something wasn't right. She had asked my older sister several times to check on me, but she didn't listen. Finally, my mum couldn't ignore her gut instinct any longer. She ran out of the church, to the car and I was sound asleep. But something told her to pick me up and take me with her. Just as she closed the car door and walked towards the church, she heard car tires screeching and saw a car crash right into the back of our car. Right where I had been asleep. Our car was a write-off.

Another time was when my brother dared me to see what my mum was cooking on the frying pan. I was only a few years old and could barely reach the top, so as I stood up to look on the stove, I grabbed hold of the panhandle, and all of the hot oil dropped on me. It poured down my chin, left shoulder, and along my arm. I suffered third-degree burns that day. There I was again, in the ICU being prayed over.

If that wasn't enough, when I was 10, the doctor told my mum that I may have a hole in my heart. I became gravely ill, but my mum sought out alternative meth-

fighting

ods and a second opinion. My poor mother. It seems I kept her on her toes from the moment I was in her womb. She said I would keep her up with my kicks and constant movement like I just wanted to burst out into the world.

My life has been fight after fight, and this is not including all the colds, fevers, broken bones, and stitches that come with being a child. My mum will testify that despite all the obstacles, none of them stopped or slowed me down in any way. It made me feel more invincible like I could take on the world.

My dad always said to me, *ma'aa le loto*. Which means rock headed in the Samoan language. I had a strong will and no fear. I think he saw a lot of himself in me, or at least I would like to think so. My father, my first superhero, comes from a lineage of chiefs and warriors. My great, great, great, grandfather, many described as a giant, he was a cannibal. Yes, he ate people, hence our name Meaola; it means living thing. However, its creation of the name connotation was animal; he was an animal. He killed and ate people, invoking fear in the hearts of many villagers and lands afar. I take on the mix; fierceness and breathing life to all around me.

My mother has an intuitive spiritual energy. She comes from a lineage of healers and intuitive foresight but don't be fooled, my mum has a wild, cheeky side. It took a real man, my dad, to embrace her. She was never too much for him. It's a love story for the ages. Some may deem it to be a bit inappropriate in today's society as they had a 20 year age difference, but it's a love they fought for.

Many may look at some of my history and perhaps feel ashamed of it. My lineage of warrior blood is steeped in cannibalism, murder, satanic rituals, and alchemy. This being banned in our religious culture and the forbidden love of a divorced man with children and a young woman, all deemed inappropriate in our conservative, traditional ways. I am so proud that woven into my DNA is a rich history of fight, adventure, wild, unconventional, forbidden, and unacceptable ways of being. It is a part of my identity that somehow, along the way, became lost in the translation of western society.

My family's history is a big part of my story, something I only recently discovered and connected with.

I grew up in Auckland, New Zealand, in a fourth-generation Christian home, a seventh-day Adventist home to be specific. I am one of sixteen siblings. Eight brothers and seven sisters. My childhood was spent being wild and free, with laughter and lots of food. These memories are so precious to me.

My father was strict, conservative, and the disciplinarian. While my mother is a sweet, beautiful woman, both of whom I adore, love, and have the utmost respect for. There is deep gratitude in my heart, a special place that belongs to my parents for who they are and who they raised me to be.

I did not come to appreciate them until I became an adult. Like most teens, I became obsessed with my self-interests. I learned the hard lessons as an adult and caught glimpses of my parents' hard work. They were immigrants from the Pacific Islands who left to seek better opportunities for themselves and future generations.

As the reader of my story, you should know, religion is a big part of my journey. It is the lens to which I will speak and refer to a lot throughout this book. It has formed the basis and foundation of my beliefs. It's shaped how I have lived, and it is also the reason for the most pivotal changes in my life, that you will see unfold throughout this book.

Along the way, something happened to the wild, sick, and young girl I once was. My love and faith in God was tested, and my life turned from an adventurous fairytale into a fight of life or death.

Let's journey together through my past challenging seasons.

2
something to prove

THE FIGHT WAS ON. With nothing to lose, you would think that would mean you wouldn't have anything to prove, but, from childhood, this was the contrary. I was constantly fighting to prove that I had what it took to do something and be someone great. I was ready to prove that at all costs, whatever it took, even if the cost was my health and soul.

I had many seasons where I was bedridden for days from sickness. You would often find me overdressed, over coddled, and over watched, because "just in case." I was always very thin and pale; it was evident that I was sick. People treated me differently because of it and felt sorry for me, but I could have fooled many. I had a fierce spirit and was always laughing. My siblings never made me feel any different. I guess that's the difference between adults and children and how we see life and each other. Adults' worldview is often filtered through life influences—health, race, religion, circumstances, protection, worry, fear, finances, whereas, with children, they just see you, a human, no filters, no perceptions.

I'm not sure where it all began and why I felt I needed to prove myself. All I knew was that I didn't want anyone's pity. I never wanted anyone's pity. Maybe subconsciously, I was sick of being sick and willed myself to wellness and stardom.

When I began school, English was my second language. I only spoke Samoan. You can just imagine what it felt like to go to school and not understand what was being said. My very first life goal was to not only speak English but to excel at it. I remember so clearly topping my class in reading that year. My heart beamed as I saw my name at the top of the classroom chart with the most stars. My spelling was outstanding. I had a thirst for books. Whether I was reading them or being read to, they brought me so much joy. Spelling tests and books were the highlights of my schooling years. I would run home after school to read to my mum. One of my fondest memories as a child was reading my mum's bible story before bed as she would rub my back. I could see how proud my mum was that I was able to read and understand it, and I craved more.

I was very popular at school, who knew that everyone would like me! I was smart, funny, and pretty good at most things. I was thriving.

As school life progressed, I found myself fighting more than I'd ever had to. There were so many smart children at school, who seemed like they had the same life goal as me, to be the best they could be. I wanted, craved more praise. The one you get when you know how well you've done on all your schoolwork because your parents, the teachers, and everyone around you affirm it. Becoming an A+ student was a huge achievement. I thought it would always be easy to receive and attain. Eventually, I learned that it took a lot of hard work to maintain that level of standard, every year for the rest of my schooling life.

The thing that frightened me the most wasn't wondering how I would maintain it. I was scared about losing the pride that my parents and teachers had for me.

From the age of four, my dad had me up on stage, in front of the church congregation, singing, playing the piano, speaking, and preaching. It became a regular part of my childhood. I felt as though I was always performing, which meant I had to be the best. Life was one big performance, and I had to be sure it was a good show.

It was hard to be a good girl all the time. I was never dainty or polite enough. I spoke too loud and too much. I was outspoken and spoke up whenever I saw injustice. I answered back and asked lots of questions. I never did what I was told. I wasn't spiritual enough. I laughed too much and was selfish. This landed me in trouble quite often, along with a few smacks.

The bigger the task, the higher the risk I took. When I saw the boys playing outside on the skateboard ramps, I would grab a skateboard and go down the mountain. If we were racing cars on the road, I would take it to the next level. I would try to beat the oncoming car to safety on my side of the road. As teenagers, we would jump off cliff tops into the quarry and to make it more thrilling, I would do it at night. It was wild, but it made me feel a sense of freedom.

I thrived being on stage, from winning speech competitions to performing arts, which took me across many stages. If that wasn't enough, I was playing sports at an elite level, travelling globally.

I did whatever it took to stay on top. I felt safe and secure there, and I often feared if I wasn't excelling or thriving, what purpose would my life have? Often my poor health would remind me how fragile I was. It was humbling on one hand, and on the other, it is what drove me not to let my health get in my way and keep striving for better.

Confidence was the key to all of it. It was my cover-up. Sometimes when I hear "fake it until you make it" or "confidence is key," I ask myself, *but is it truly enough?* Being witty and outspoken was me trying to cover up what I didn't have or what I only wanted people to see. The thing is, you become so good at lying to yourself that it almost feels real. I felt as though I was unstoppable but not in the best way. Fighting to stay at the top of my own disillusioned game required lying, cheating, manipulation, coercion, deceit, rebellion, disobedience, and downright dirty shame. I thought it was worth it at the time, selling my soul to the devil for momentary self-gratification. I had something to prove, even at the cost of my health or, in this case, my soul.

Some may say this isn't a fight in the literal sense of the word, but I say if it's a cause important to you, and you are doing whatever it takes to make it happen, against all the odds, then that's a fight in every sense of the word. You understand the battle between being your true self and being the self that seeks validation from others.

3

perfection has its price

I MARRIED YOUNG. Twenty years old, to be exact. I had been dating Ken, my sweetheart, for eight years already; we had grown up together. We were neighbours and family friends. It was the opposite of love at first sight, I hated him, and he never liked me either. I was stuck up, and I thought he was into men. Neither of us imagined that we would make amazing partners and be soulmates. Getting married felt like the next logical step in our relationship.

If you're a sucker for extravagant proposals, sorry to disappoint you, but ours wasn't one. It went more of something like this...

I said, "Soooo, hey, should we just get married?" and he said, "It feels like that's the right thing to do, right?" According to him, this means technically I proposed to him.

We were in this relationship for the long haul. We had migrated together from New Zealand to Australia to make a new life for ourselves, so it didn't seem like a crazy idea. Maybe, it was code that things had gone a bit stale in our relationship.

I wonder where we get that kind of thinking from? The thought that when your relationship is feeling stale or boring, it means you need to make a significant life change, get married, have a baby, buy a house, move to another country.

No matter the reason there, I was, at the altar, marrying the man I committed to eight years prior. I can still recall every romantic movie, fantasy dream, and religious counselling we had been given. Life to come was going to be so grand.

We moved into our little two-bedroom flat, and that's when it hit me, I didn't have a razoo on what it meant to be a wife. I couldn't cook, hated cleaning, hated chores, oh and hated my job. I found all those things boring and mundane. Nobody ever taught me or showed me how to please my husband.

He came home expecting the house to be clean and food cooked but, that wasn't the reality. I asked myself, *How have we been together for so long, and I don't know any of this?*

The first year of marital bliss was anything but. I believe we would have gotten a divorce had I not found out I was pregnant. *What does he expect of me?* I thought this to myself constantly. Where in the marriage contract did it say that I had to do his laundry, iron, cook, clean, have and raise the children, and have sex whenever he wanted, all while he had a nap, kicked up his feet, and did nothing. Just because I stayed home all day and did nothing while he went to work. I was livid. On top of that, I was depressed. I hated my fat body, swollen feet, thighs, hands, face, almost everything about myself. I couldn't fit into my clothes anymore. I thought that being fat was a normal part of being pregnant; I just couldn't stop eating, which only made me more depressed.

I wanted control. I wanted my way. I argued and fought with Ken. I cried and cried some more, ate, and ate some more. It was a downward spiral, and I was over it. Even more, I was over him.

But I had Jesus, Jesus is the answer. Right?

But where was he? Where were my spiritual guides, mentors, and friends? I felt betrayed and disillusioned by everyone around me who portrayed some level of this marital myth and perfect dream. Or maybe, I was completely ignorant, selfish, and short-sighted. Whichever one it was, it didn't matter. I was ready to exit my marriage and give my child away at birth.

On October 2, 2003, my baby boy Jireh was born. I couldn't help but just stare at him that first night as he slept in the cot next to me. All I could do was watch him while he slept; I was in awe. *How did we create this perfect creature?* He instantly became the apple of my eye; he was perfect. Then he began to cry, and I looked around, calling for the nurse.

I pushed the buzzer, and as the nurse entered the room, I told her, "Help, he's crying!"

"Yes, that's what babies do, and it's up to you to do something about it." She replied.

What! I just gave birth. I'm exhausted. Isn't that your job? How do I, what do I do?

I was confused and felt the betrayal once again. Out of every romantic movie I had ever watched, none had told a realistic tale. My expectations were shot instantly. I cried; I didn't know what to do. There was no manual and no one to guide me. It was "fend for yourself." I felt helpless and hopeless all at once.

That night I vowed to myself that I would make it work, I could do it, raise my baby, and be a good mum to overcome the odds just like I did as a child. I grew up feeling as though I was on my own. I was not to rely on anyone as *everyone will only disappoint you*. It was up to me to protect, love, care for, and do everything for my child. No one was going to be there for me, to do it for me, or to tell me how it's done. I had so many moments growing up where I realized I was resilient and could get through anything. Here I was facing another turning point in my journey in the hospital room. It felt like not only was my son born that day but I, too, was reborn.

We returned from the hospital and moved back into my parent's home. We welcomed help and wisdom from my mum, dad, grandma, and siblings to raise Jireh. They were all so amazing and loved him immensely. But I didn't forget my vow. Therefore, it was my duty and responsibility as his mother to give him the best of the best. And just like that, superwoman or super Mum, as many affectionately called me, was born. A true hero in a mother's apron. Survival mode and perfectionism kicked into overdrive, hyperdrive. I was determined.

When Jireh was one year old, we bought our first home, where we lived together with my parents and siblings. Here, I set a new standard for myself. I began writing the manual I never had about being the perfect mother and wife—going the extra mile to cook everything from scratch and having a vegetarian diet. Thank you, Pinterest! We had the finest furniture, clean home, pristinely ironed garments, and polished ornaments. I became a hospitality guru.

I was ministering to married couples, young mothers, and upcoming young girls. I was never tired or exhausted. Praise flooded in, and I felt I was on a pedestal, which only fed my ego and cravings for external validation. On the outside, everything was perfect and positive; life was bliss. I made everything look easy, and I never stressed. I just did what had to be done. But, I had created this delusional reality. Next to my cleanliness was godliness. My children were so well mannered, and as they grew up, I began homeschooling them. The house was always clean, we were popular and well respected in our community. We had money, and our schedule was like clockwork, not a hair out of place except it wasn't real.

Behind closed doors, I was addicted to cleaning and making sure everything looked perfect. I was anxious that I wouldn't meet my self-set standard. Afraid to be caught off guard by someone outside of our home. If things weren't perfect, my anxiety arose. I manipulated my surroundings not to feel my anxiety and to manage my addiction without losing control. My temper was short. My need for perfection was out of control. I had to keep up the show, even if it was at the expense of my

perfection has its price

health. Ken only fed my obsession. He loved having a trophy wife. He loved order, cleanliness, and structure just as much, if not more, than I did. He was thriving in the environment. His boastful words would feed my ego. He had his own obsession and addiction, having everything looking and working perfectly. A perfect match to thrive, I never slept and purposely created insomnia.

I didn't know how to save myself from myself. I happily treaded this way for many years. I honestly believed I could keep going this way. In my eyes, I was *slaying* the adult game. Eventually, the shine wore off, a familiar feeling of discontentment and dissatisfaction of achieving all that could be achieved in womanhood began to loom over me. As much as I had come to love my perfect life, the thoughts of adventure and the wild side began to call my heart. I constantly asked myself, *how do I get out of this game?* I was bored again. It was a different feeling of failure. I now had some kind of experience and success. So why was I feeling so unfulfilled? I felt more trapped than ever.

4

too beautiful for this earth

IT IS ONE THING TO BE AWARE that the life you are living no longer serves you and another to know what to do about it. My will and fight were strong. I truly believed that if I willed myself enough to change something, it would happen. But my will was not enough to fight off the ever-growing feelings of helplessness and despair I was beginning to feel.

On January 18, 2005, we welcomed our second baby into the world, Ezreh, weighing 10lbs. After giving birth, things took a turn for the worse because I was losing blood. I had to be rushed to the ICU. I didn't realize until later how dangerous the situation was and how close I came to dying that day. Today, we joke with Ezreh that it was because of his big head.

It was fascinating to see the difference in personalities between Jireh and Ezreh when they were first born. Jireh was fussy and demanding while Ezreh was placid and slept through the night.

When Ezreh was born, I decided to change things up and went into the ministry to do missionary work. I convinced myself that this would be more fulfilling and purposeful.

That it was exactly what I needed to get out of the boring and mundane day to day life I felt I had conquered. As always, I dived into this idea, head first, and began to change everything around me to make it work.

We came up with a plan to renovate and sell our house to pay off our debts and begin fresh with a clean slate. We then headed to Victoria to help out and support our Pastor's friends with their church ministry. As we talked more about it, the more excited we were. We felt this was *the way*.

I didn't realize how slow the process of renovating and selling a house would be. That it would take and require something from me that I had zero tolerance for—patience! I tried to hurry the process with zeal, pestering, whining, and complaining. I needed Ken to hurry up with the renovations and get our house sold.

It felt like everything was happening too slowly. In my eyes, he was not doing enough after work or on his days off. I was on the clock and wanted everything done so I could move onto the next thing.

During this time, I began to get sick. Morning sickness, and I couldn't have been more devastated. *I don't have time for this!* I prayed and pleaded with God for a miscarriage.

For the first 12 weeks, I couldn't accept the pregnancy. I hoped that I would lose the baby before it was a *real baby*. I cried every night. By the 16th week of pregnancy, I slowly concluded that this baby was here, and I just had to accept it.

At my 18-week ultrasound scan, I found out that I was having a girl. I walked out of the radiology room that day, over the moon. *I'm having a girl!* My first daughter. Everything changed as I embraced having a little girl. I began to prepare for her arrival. We had to make room and create a new plan that included her with her brothers. We continued renovating, baby preparing and my impatience for the home renovations seemed to be on pause.

July 2006 came around, and the impending birth was near as I was already 40 weeks pregnant. Plans were put on hold as we decided to have her first, but we kept the house on the market as we knew it would take time. "At least when it sold, she will be here with us," we thought to ourselves.

The day before she arrived, we spent the day at the aquarium with my family. It was a beautiful busy day. A thought crossed my mind while we were out, *I haven't felt the baby move much.* I mentioned it to Ken, but he brushed it off as me being paranoid. *That I was!* We carried on with our day, and as we arrived home, the thought came back. To get my mind off it, I decided it was a good time to scrub my kitchen floor, on my hands and knees. It needed a good polishing.

As I got into bed, I drank a cold glass of water and felt her move. Or so I believed. I couldn't escape that initial thought, that I hadn't felt her move most of the day. I tossed and turned all night.

The morning she arrived was a haze.

Ken had gone off to work, and I got up an hour later to go to the bathroom. I was exhausted. As I looked up from the toilet, I saw a murky green colour that looked like vomit, all over the bathroom floor. I hadn't noticed that it came out of me. I could feel it everywhere, and I thought to myself, *this cannot be good.* Contractions began, and I called Ken to come home immediately.

For the next couple of hours, everything seemed to be one big blur. From the time they told me I was going into labour, to the time they said there was a very faint heartbeat to my daughter. To seeing the flatline on the ultrasound screen, to seeing her lifeless body on my stomach. I just endured an 18-hour labour, only to birth my lifeless baby, who wouldn't be coming home with me.

I cannot describe what those 18 hours were like. My first thought was, "God promises he will never allow anything to come to you that you are not able to endure." I repeated that promise over and over again, knowing and trusting that somehow I would get through. Instantly, there were so many thoughts and regrets. The strength of my faith came powering in. I was surrounded by love and my beautiful community. It was like being in a sweet torture chamber; if there is such a thing.

On July 17, 2006, our baby girl, Zion Angel, came into the world weighing 14 lbs, and she was the most perfect girl I had ever seen. My heart just exploded with love. My Zion Angel was too beautiful for this earth.

My husband and I spent hours after her birth cradling her in our arms. My mum brought in our boys and our best friends, so they could see her before they had to take her from us. That night, I wrapped my arms around my stomach and wailed over my childless womb, not having my baby to stare at all night as I had with my first two. I wasn't sure how I could endure the pain. For the first few weeks, I went to sleep, pining for her. Somehow, I managed to prepare for her funeral. I was solid in my faith, yet felt numb. My natural default was to put on another show, not daring to delve into my emotions. I was afraid that I was not being faithful or a good enough Christian.

When we buried her, I lost a big piece of my heart. I didn't realize that this experience would be the first of many losses that were to come. I never questioned God; I never doubted him. I never wanted an autopsy to know why. I just trusted. Perhaps I was only faithful to my faith that never faltered. I was a testimony, an example of what that should look like.

5

season of loss

I HAD MADE IT THROUGH MY MARTYR EXPERIENCE. *Oh lord, who could endure losing their child?*

I was in for a rude awakening. I had read and heard about all of these stories of real-life encounters how one's faith was strengthened. I truly believed that my one experience was sufficient to turn me into the kind of person many could look up to. I grieved for the first few weeks but then went right back to where I left off. Selling our home and going to do missionary work. We had lost our first opportunity with our pastoral friends because time had elapsed, and so I was out seeking a new one.

As I reflect now, perhaps this was what grieving or coping looked like to me. I could see a change in my husband, as well. He decided to change the renovation plans so that the home would have more value. This project took and tested my patience on new levels and took our marriage to the brink. We rebuilt a completely different house. It took us three years before we put it on the market for the second time.

During that time, we welcomed baby number four. I didn't want another child after we lost Zion, especially a girl. The moment we found out I would be having a girl, the uncertainty settled in. I was more careful and mindful of everything I did during my pregnancy this time around. I made sure to show myself love and care. As her due date approached, I could feel the fear and anxiety looming over me. I had many conversations with God about her birth, praying for protection and strength. I spoke to him about my fears of losing another child. My heart couldn't bear another loss. The doctors believed it would be safest for the baby. To induce her four weeks early. Safety sounded good to me.

On March 7th, 2008, at 6:00 am, we arrived at the hospital and began the induction process. Labour was extremely long. As I breathed my way through the artificial contractions, each coming at quick paces and with intense rhythms, the monitor and regular check-ins assured me that my baby girl's heartbeat was stable and strong. I continued to pray and recite God's promises throughout the labour. At 11:00 pm, Rehnee Eden came roaring into this world. It took a deep breath, a push that sounded like a roar, and there she was; 8 lbs of perfection. As I held her on my chest, my heart was in pure elation; I burst into joyful tears for her safe birth and, at the same time, mourned for her sister Zion who wasn't there.

I lost a bit of blood post-birth, a hemorrhage that required a blood transfusion. Rehnee had to go to the newborn nursery, and while there, she became unwell. We found out she had sepsis, a life-threatening blood infection, and had to go to the NICU. A few days later, I was discharged from the hospital, but Rehnee wasn't able to come home with me, which triggered the painful memory of walking out of the hospital without Zion. I refused to be separated. I fought to stay by her side, but with the hospital policy and Rehnee's condition, I had to trust she was in good hands. But ultimately, I was devastated.

I would get to the hospital early and stay all day long. I only went home to sleep. That is what my days looked like for two weeks until she came home with us two weeks later. I was so thankful that they caught the infection early. My fondest memory of Rehnee during her time in the NICU was when she was finally able to feed. The nurses said, "Jen, she's such a stubborn one, a fighter, this one!" She would never take the bottle of my breast milk; she wanted it directly from me. She would scream, fuss, and cry the whole time until I got there to feed her. She is my only daughter in our mob, and she's so precious to us.

Our house had only been on the market for several months, but Ken was not happy with the going rate, so we took our home off the market. We decided to continue our travels and renovations. Another year went by, and it seemed to be another year of up levelling. While in the background, I continued to homeschool the kids, host parties (even through renovations), and buy things that I didn't need. It was like being in the same trap; it just somehow looked and felt different.

2010 was approaching, and I started wondering where time had gone. I questioned what I had achieved to date. I was bored, and the urge to make drastic changes began to settle in. I was done.

We finally found a new missionary opportunity. It was the one we had been in search of for the last five years. Once again, we put our house on the market. Lucky number three, right? At least that's what we thought.

season of loss

It was Sunday, February 28, 2010, a day I will never forget; we had an open house scheduled. At the end of the open house, we were given an irresistible offer, which we accepted. The buyer was coming the next morning to sign the paperwork. We were feeling excited and relieved as we went to bed that night. Our hard work was coming to an end, and an exciting new chapter was waiting for us.

The next morning, Ken left for work at 5:00 am, and I got up around 6:30 am. I slept in that morning because I deserved it. I could smell a strong stench, and as I glided down my hallway, admiring my immaculately clean home, I couldn't tell where the stench was coming from. I went out the back but couldn't see anything. So I went back inside and touched up a few things before the boys and Rehnee got up. I began preparing for the buyer, who was coming at 11:00 am. By then, it was 7:00 am. I went to the bathroom and heard a scratching noise coming from the ceiling.

Oh no, please don't tell me there are mice in the house, not today, I thought to myself. As I looked up at the small bathroom fan in the ceiling, I saw flames! *Flames?* There was fire! I leaped up so fast, screamed fire as I ran down the hallways to wake up my kids. My sister and brother who were visiting had slept over, and upon hearing, my screams shouted, *fire, everyone get out!*

I began to hear car horns going off and neighbours yelling as we all ran out the front door. I was begging the Lord, *please, please let this be a dream, please don't let this be happening to all our hard work, please, please!* As our family got outside safely, I turned around and saw our entire roof was on fire. The neighbours had called the fire services, and I decided it would be a good idea to run back in and get all our valuable documents and photos. I ran down the hallway and tried to get in the room where I stored them, but that room was completely on fire, so I had no choice but to leave them behind and run back outside. But then I realized I forgot to call Ken, so I ran back into the house. *Honey, you have to come home now. The house is on fire. No, this is not a joke!* I can't believe he thought I was joking. I hung up the phone. Everyone was yelling at me to get out of the house. Just as I ran out, the entire middle of the house collapsed, and as I watched, I collapsed along with it.

I was outside, hugging my kids, crying, and watching our home burn down right in front of my eyes. The fire was ferocious, it consumed everything, and it took the firefighters a while to put the fire out. As Ken arrived, so did our friends, and our real estate agent, only to watch with us, crying, but not knowing how to feel or what to say.

season of loss

The next few moments felt like one giant moment. The generosity and love we felt from our loved ones and community was so heartwarming. We slept at my mum's place the first night. We were not in a very good place with my family, so it felt uncomfortable to stay. The next night, our insurance company made arrangements for us to stay in a hotel, and we began to put together a plan. My mind never stopped. I kept thinking about what had to happen next. What *now? What's the solution?* My faith always guided me, and during this time, it was shining through.

For the most part, I was ok. They were just things, all replaceable, just a hassle. We were supposed to be leaving to go into missionary work, and I wasn't going to allow this to stop me. *What can we do?* I thought to myself. The reality is, there wasn't anything we could do about the house. We had to let the insurance sort things out as we continued with our plan.

We received the fire inspectors report a few days later. The chief firefighter on scene the day of the fire was telling me they were confident that I didn't start the fire myself or tried to burn my family inside the house. We laughed a bit, as he was joking, but he quickly turned serious to say that it was quite common for mothers to do so. I was shocked!

We already had an idea how the fire had started. Earlier in the month, we had our evaporative cooling system installed, which meant the tradesmen were up inside the attic of our home, which was also our storage place as well. We thought perhaps the tradesmen had installed something faulty. What the inspector found was that one of our plastic storage bags had been moved and placed on the transformer which was the source that powers light.

The night before, of our final open home inspection, I was exhausted. I went to bed, and I had forgotten to turn off the light switch in our laundry room. It then heated up the bag that was on top of the transformer, catching fire and spreading to the insulation in the ceiling and everything else stored up there.

Indirectly, I felt it was my fault. I had forgotten to turn off the light in our laundry room. I was the last one up, to lock up, and make sure everything was turned off. For months, I felt terribly guilty. Just the thought that a fire was burning in the ceiling all night and the firefighter telling me that our sense of smell shuts down while we sleep. Which is why night fires are deadly. These thoughts replayed in my mind for months following, it was traumatizing.

A week later, my dad had a stroke and was admitted to the hospital.

season of loss

We were playing in the pool when we received the devastating phone call. At any time, my father could pass. We knew it was coming. But there was no way to prepare for that deep of a loss. My heart was not ready to say goodbye to my Dad; my first love and superhero. We arrived at the hospital, just as he took his last breath. His face was still warm as I rushed in and hugged him for the last time. I crumpled into my brother's arms; we were devastated.

As we drove back to our temporary home, things came into perspective. I had just lost my home and monetary things, all those could be replaced but also a life that couldn't be replaced. My heart was broken. I remember wailing on my bed that night, the same way I wailed the night I lost Zion. A cry of pure pain and agony for the loss of a life so precious to me. I think some of the hotel guests complained to reception about the noise, but I didn't care. I was in mourning. His funeral was the saddest day of my life. I was sure that I wouldn't recover.

The night after the funeral, we continued with our plan to dive into missionary work and left to go to a family camp. We then headed to the drug and rehabilitation centre, where we would start our work. I was determined as ever to not allow the obstacles to stop me from pursuing my life's calling.

The next few scenes happened in succession, like a big fireball, that started small and only got bigger and bigger. We fought on, in our new place of the missionary, travelling all around Australia, helping youth at risk through adventure therapy. Adventure therapy is an experiential approach to healing through adventure and recreational activities mixed with trust and team building activities, small group discussions, journaling and healing in a safe, supportive environment run mostly outdoors. This experience was amazing.

On our travels, we found out I was pregnant again. It was not the best pregnancy, however. I went into labour very early, from the stress and grief of losing my dad, and birthed a premature baby at 33 weeks. Reymah was born on August 08, 2010. In every way, he reminds me so much of my dad, his hair, the shape of his mouth, the way he eats, his smile, his personality, his magnetism draws everyone to him, just like my dad. Reymah was in the hospital for the next eight weeks. When he was discharged from the hospital, I took him straight to the camp we were staying at.

We were still fighting with the insurance company from our fire home to get the house rebuilt. In that time, we decided it was best to rent a house on a short term lease, instead of living at a caravan park jumping from hotel to hotel. It had only been a couple of months

season of loss

there when someone from the city council called us and told us that we only had 24 hours to get our stuff out of our rental home as there had been a landslide. Our home was right in the middle of the danger zone. The house had already moved. The hill below it had a landslid, and our driveway had caved in. Our community workmates filled it with a bulldozer as we got out as much as we could, but still, we had to leave most of our possessions behind. Yet again, we lost another home, and I lost more of my heart.

With nowhere to call home, we were back at a caravan park around the corner from the drug and rehab centre. Even though we were travelling a bit for our work, we still needed a base camp, so we stayed there temporarily until our old fire home's rebuilding began. When the house was still being finished, we decided to move into the back section to save money temporarily. It had been a year since the fire when the house was completed, and as it finished, we put it straight back on the market again for the fourth time.

It was 2011, and Melbourne was hit with floods. Our fire home was ruined once again. The whole rebuilding process began again. We continued with out work, which became challenging on every level. It challenged my faith personally. Adventure therapy as a facilitator requires a deep level of truth and surrender, something, at this time, I didn't believe I had. It confronted me with some of my own beliefs that conflicted with how the program was run. I was forever questioning, learning, and being thrown out of my comfort zone, so many of the young people's lives we were encountering changed how I thought and lived out in the world, a life-transforming experience, real stories that changed my life!

Fifteen months after Reymah was born, we had another baby boy, Torah. Each pregnancy and birth seemed like a haze by this stage. We were going through so much all at the same time. I found it hard to experience joy while processing the challenges surrounding my life. Torah's birth was also induced, just like Rehnee. It was another long, difficult labour. After 25 hours in labour, the doctors pulled the plug and said I had to have an emergency c-section. Despite Torah's strong heartbeat, the intensity of induction can be a fight. All of my prior births had been natural, so to have an emergency c-section, just felt like another injustice mounting up. I felt like I failed Torah by having a c-section because I viewed caesareans as the wrong way a baby should come into this world. I worried about the complications and how this would implicate our family. I knew about all of the negative health risks of having a c-section, so because of this, I fought so hard to have him naturally, but it wasn't happening.

Once again, I lost a lot of blood, another hemorrhage. There we went again with a blood transfusion and separation from my baby for the first few hours. It felt like the first 72 hours of Torah's birth were a blur. Once I was discharged, I had another six weeks of recovery. No driving, no exercise, lift nothing but your baby. I couldn't deal with it anymore. I struggled to recover physically post Torah's birth. Even to this day, I'm not able to lose weight as quickly, and that has weighed on my self-worth and health.

As we continued through our missionary work, Torah turned two, and we decided to move to Western Australia to live and work in indigenous communities. Finally, after the fifth time of rebuilding our home, it sold. We headed to where we believed would be our fresh start.

Arriving in Western Australia was a dream come true. I felt as though we were where we were meant to be. Everything we had gone through felt like it had been worth it to end up there. It was the best time, until tragedy struck, again.

In June of 2013, we were in a car accident, everyone was ok, but I had injured my lumbar spine and had to be flown to the hospital in a helicopter, 12 hours away. We were in the middle of the desert, and the main hospital was in the big city. I didn't see my husband and kids for months. As I underwent care and rehabilitation, I opted not to have an operation, which was a significant risk due to any kind of nerve damage that could have rendered me paralyzed for the rest of my life. And to my surprise, I also found out I was in the early stages of pregnancy with baby number six. Having an operation was not an option. I'd take the risk to physically rehabilitate even if it meant that it was going to take much longer. I remember lying still on that hospital bed for weeks, feeling alone, in pain, and out of control.

The last ten years of my life flashed before my eyes. This was the turning point. This was the moment I would remember and come back to. It was the moment that made everything I had done, all that had happened, and everything I believed in up until that point change forever.

The moment where all the walls, all the masks, everything that had kept me safe for so long, came crumbling down. I cried out to God, "Lord, help me, I am done! If you don't show me who you are, or that you can save me, I am done, that's it, I'm turning away" I was left with nothing, I felt nothing, and I wanted nothing. I lived for nothing. This was the first moment I remember that I was going to give up. But then God spoke to me. It was crystal clear, like a two-way conversation.

"Do you honestly want to know who I am, not just know about me, but know me? Ok, here I come!"

6

falling short

THOSE WORDS INSTANTLY gave me a sense of relief. Perhaps it was a hallucination or a side effect from the strong medication I was under, but in my heart, I knew it to be him. I don't think I'd ever recalled hearing his voice before. As a child, I was never taught that God speaks to you. I interpreted what he said to me as everything would be smooth sailing from here on out, my season of struggle and hardship was done, over. Surely it had to be.

I had a renewed perspective and a refreshed mindset. Even from my hospital bed, in pain, on my own, 12 hours away from my husband and children, I slept soundly for the first time in the longest time. For two straight weeks, I was in and out of consciousness, and I thought, "I could get used to this." I was having conversations with God, reading my bible, and enjoying the rare quiet time. I saw it as an opportunity.

I didn't mind this. As an insomniac, I welcomed the rest. I couldn't recall the last time before this that my mind and body got much-needed sleep. I guess the heavy medication I was under also influenced my exhaustion in keeping me as comfortable as possible.

For the first few weeks of being in the hospital, I was bound to my bed, unable to move or get up. There was too much inflammation, and my x-rays were never accurate. It was a waiting game. I had barely spoken a word to Ken and the kids because I was so out of it. A blood clot started to form in my right leg. My heavily bruised stomach and chest were in for more bruising from the stomach injections to thin my blood.

After the first few weeks of enjoying rest, reality hit me. The feeling of helplessness began to stir within me. I yearned for my family. I craved to have a shower, eat a decent meal, and just get up and move. I wanted to do what needed to be done so that I could get out of there. I tried to be strong and focus on being patient, but it was hard.

falling short

Oftentimes, I would scream out in the middle of the night in agony and grief. I spent every day crying and crying, begging for someone to help me. I felt like all my cries and screams were never heard. I would punch the bed and fistfight the air to let out my frustration. I was crying out to God for help.

I spoke and reflected a lot. My life continued to flash before my eyes, almost like a movie, except watching my life playback. There were so many painful memories and moments that I missed. I tried to recall the timeline of my adult life but couldn't remember much at all.

I felt confronted. I began going through old photos on my phone and found myself struggling to remember. How could I have been there, but not remember? I was living life on autopilot, and it finally caught up with me. Being in the hospital ended the autopilot mode I was in and forced me to stop and slow down. But it didn't stop me from wanting to speed up the recovery process.

Like clockwork, I knew when the doctors were coming. I tried to be presentable, often feeling ashamed of my appearance, bad breath, and partially naked self. Just like I did as a child, I asked many questions, "what's next, what can we do, how can I get better faster?" I would plead with them to help me as I just wanted to go home.

I had to make the most of my time in the hospital. I knew every nurse's name and would buzz them for just about everything so that they would come, and I could have a conversation. I read countless magazines and asked for every book in their library to read. I watched TV until my brain felt like it was no longer functioning, and I didn't have the brain capacity to think or feel optimistic about anything.

After the first month, my physical testing and rehabilitation began. My level of joy went up a notch because going home felt within reach. My first day up and out of bed consisted of me being assisted with my first shower, which looked like me sitting on a chair being washed by the nurse. As if I wasn't humiliated already, this took it to the next level. Then, my first trip to the bathroom and not being able to wipe my own bottom was an all-time low. I cried for days accepting this part of my recovery.

Finally, the scans and x-rays came back. It turned out that my lumbar spine was fractured, not broken. It wasn't the best news, but still, the better of the two. Lumbar spine fractures and breaks aren't an easy recovery. It is said that it is the trickiest part of the back to rehabilitate and heal once damaged. I was told that I would heal but that I would be experiencing chronic pain for the rest of my life and be on medication. They said that physical rehab would take a long time before I was back to 100%, but for me, this gave me hope and light. The time in the hospital was feeling dark so having a bit of light is what I needed.

At every session with my rehab team, I pushed myself the extra mile more than what was expected of me. I had to learn how to walk, move, and do things for myself, and it was excruciating. We started with hydrotherapy, which had me put in a wheelchair and lowered into the water. In the beginning, I felt humiliated and ashamed. And to top that off, my physiotherapist was good looking, which made me feel more embarrassed when he had to take me out from the wheelchair and carry me. I eventually got over myself, and we exchanged wonderful conversations during our sessions.

It felt like I went from being a thriving mother and wife to nothing. I had no control over my circumstances. No matter how hard I prayed, I couldn't do a damn thing about it.

If you think physiotherapy was enough, I also had to see a psychologist, and the sessions were brutal. I didn't like psychologists, and I felt I certainly didn't need one. I was skeptical and thought they had ill intentions. It felt like they were waiting for me to slip up so that they could put me in a loony bin. But as it turned out, my psychologist was terrific. I could not deny how much I needed to talk about everything I had been through and how much I was able to release. It wasn't just that, but also being able to identify the areas of my life that had been serving me. I looked forward to those sessions; who would've known?

I had been in the hospital already for over a month, and I started to miss my kids deeply. I wondered what they were doing, and if they were ok. I spoke to them daily and held back tears because we weren't together. I pined for them day and night. I had nightmares that I failed them, that they needed me, and I wasn't there for them.

At the same time, I kept forgetting that I was pregnant. I always had terrible morning sickness during my pregnancies, other than feeling that and seeing my stomach grow; it was the last thought on my mind. I was starving, as well. Having medication and morning sickness made me feel even worse. I couldn't keep any food down, plus the pain just exacerbated my feelings of helplessness.

Every day it was the same mundane routine, and no surprise, I was so over it. A few months later, once I got to the point of doing basic movements for myself and didn't have to have 24-hour monitoring, they transferred me from the critical care unit to the physical rehabilitation hospital. Which was just a different wing in the hospital where hospital rooms felt like tiny apartments. It was a refreshing change to my recovery and mental health.

I began to feel a bit more alive and clearer in my thought process. It had been months since I picked up my bible, so I started reading and praying again. We had our personalized rehabilitation program to follow but could also join group sessions. I had neighbours! Finally, other patients I could see and spend time with. The hospital tried to make the long road to recovery as pleasant as possible; it was amazing.

I met some beautiful people that became close friends who were on the same journey as me. Thank God for the change in scenery because I'm not sure how much longer I would have lasted in my hospital room; I was losing it. These new connections and community gave me life. We laughed together, rehabbed together, had movie nights, and openly shared our struggles (and lots of food).

They were all local to Perth, so their families would come to visit. Although I didn't have visits, they included me in their family visits. I hadn't seen Ken and the kids for almost four months. Those visits didn't replace how much I missed my family, but they immediately became my family. It's a perfect example of how having a community can change one's life.

They bought me new clothes when my clothes started not to fit. There was always gossip about some of the specialists that we liked and disliked, and also about other patients; one of the girls was having an affair with one of the doctors. This was how we would pass the time frivolity over each other's personal lives.

The only time we felt like patients was while doing our programs, blood pressure checks, x-rays, scans, and taking medication. They wanted us to feel some kind of normality in our apartments, a home away from home.

The plan was to be at the hospital for the whole ten months of my pregnancy. They believed this would help my recovery and also after I had the baby, I would need extra rehabilitation. Ken made the call to no longer be separated from each other. So, we made a new plan. We had my rehabilitation and care transferred to Melbourne. As much as I was over the moon to be seeing Ken and our children again, I was not ready to go back to Melbourne. Too much had happened there, and I felt at least in Perth I was making progress. I was on a spiritual high. Not only was I recovering from my back injury, but I felt that for the first time mentally and emotionally, I was in a better place.

I was nowhere near full recovery. I continued intense physical rehabilitation for two years, but the internal healing took even longer. When we arrived back in

Melbourne, I had to wait for an inpatient room, so we returned to my mum's home.

The thing is, I never told my family that we had a car accident and that I had been in the hospital for the last few months. I made my sister promise not to tell anyone. She stayed with my family during this time, and it was the biggest blessing for our family. She came to visit and ended up helping Ken watch the kids while I was away in the hospital, which gave me a level of comfort. She is a wonderful sister, one of my best friends, and I am eternally grateful for the role she played here during this season and still does in my life today.

My family had no idea we were even coming back home until we just showed up on their doorstep. My mum saw me barely able to walk and with a growing belly as I was now five months pregnant. We stayed there until I got my placement at the hospital. From there, we moved into our new home, which was around the corner from the hospital.

The rehab program was kept the same but being back in Melbourne and my healing took a strange turn. I spiralled downwards into a dark despair; my progress was slow and was taking far too long, for the old impatient me. I had so much coming up that I struggled to move forward. I tried to cut myself slack because I was pregnant and spent most of my days lying in bed. Being bedridden was a nightmare for me. It meant a loss of control, and I regressed quite severely.

Four months later, I went from one hospital ward to the maternity ward and gave birth to my baby boy number five, Neareh. We named him after my experience with God.

His birth mirrored my previous children's birth, traumatic and with heavy medical intervention. This birth was a little bit more unique, given that I had a broken back. I was only able to give birth one way, on my back, which ironically seemed to be the most comfortable. His induction birth was long and physically challenging, but spiritually I felt and believed that God was in control. The fear and anxiety were so real; this birth had a bit of everything happening all at once. Somehow, I had him naturally but bled again, just like my previous labours, and had to have a blood transfusion. Neareh was sent to a special nursery due to jaundice. Separated once again from my baby, and I was devastated. One thing after another, a never-ending climb up a mountain, and I didn't know how much more my heart could take.

After Neareh was discharged, we bought him home, and I was in awe of my family. I struggled to connect with Neareh, not because of him, but because of everything I was dealing with. It was during one of my sessions with my psychologist that I realized that, for the first time, I was experiencing postpartum depression. My body wasn't at it's best, and I couldn't give him the nourishment he needed, even while breastfeeding.

There I was a mum of six, dealing with grief and trauma built up from previous years, postpartum depression, post-traumatic stress disorder from the accident, and an obsessive-compulsive disorder. It was a recipe for disaster. I didn't know where I was, who I was, or what day it was. My mental health was suffering. My memory was terrible and basic self-care went out the window. I was crying, cussing, and filled with rage daily. I had no motivation for anything and spent most of my days in bed.

Who had I become?

I had glimpses of my old self. The driven part of me told me; *keep going; you're not trying hard enough. Get moving; you can do it. You aren't done here yet.* My burning desire was strong, but my body and mind were still so weak.

Ken became my full-time caregiver. Working hard labour is all he's known. From the age of 14, he became a workaholic, and now that would be put on hold to take care of the children and me. Through everything that's happened, I never stopped to look at life from his perspective or to consider how he may have been feeling. I never considered what he might have been going through. But, this happened to me right, not him. He had it easy. I had a sense of entitlement that he had to do for me what I could not do for myself, and I didn't want him asking anyone for help. This was his duty and responsibility. For the most part, he did a fantastic job. He was trying his best to help me recover, but in my eyes, he was falling short. I resented him.

Reluctantly, I agreed that it would be best for the children to go back to school because he couldn't homeschool them. I was frustrated because he knew how much it meant to me that they were homeschooled. More was being taken away, and I was broken. Ken and I switched places, and our family unit was suffering. There was no discipline, and the house wasn't being kept clean. The children were watching too many movies, and every now and then, Ken would lose his temper and lash out. *If only this didn't happen to me, things wouldn't be this way.*

My need to heal and recover became my addiction. The more I craved this, the more helpless I felt. I called out to the Lord for his healing and mercy. I called out for help. *Why is no one helping me?* No one came over to ask us if we were ok. No one called or sent a message. No one offered to help or support us. I was devastated. I know I told Ken not to ask for help, but it had to be common sense for people to offer to help. Could they not see what was happening here?

My family was there for us from time to time; at least they tried to be, especially my sisters. But where was our church? Where were our friends? It is during times like these that you come to know who your real friends are. And I clearly had none. We had moved back to Melbourne for support and help, but we were better off back in the desert. There was only one family that helped us, and if you ever read this, thank you. I will never forget your kindness. You helped me heal physically and, in some ways, spiritually through your gift and service.

I had to confront my harsh reality. Not being able to do a thing about it was depressing. My will was growing weary, my faith dry, and I began entertaining very real thoughts that nothing was worth living for. I wasn't worth it anyway; my family would just be better off if I weren't here. I was becoming a burden. I was of no use. I hit rock bottom. For the first time, I could admit that I was defeated.

I never thought I could go into the darkest parts of my mind, where there was no light. I pleaded with God to not wake me up in the mornings because I could no longer bear to see another sunrise or another useless day of nothing but trying to heal and get better. That never worked, because I never slept. The insomnia was real; the pain kept me up. Most nights were spent listening to my racing mind, and I still had a newborn baby that I had to care for but wasn't able to. I continued to breastfeed him, but I was exhausted and tormented all at the same time, bound in my head.

I didn't understand what God meant when he had spoken to me while I was in the hospital bed up in Perth. I still desired that relief. It seemed so distant now. I separated myself from everyone. Even from my children, I did not want to deal with the guilt that I had failed and let them down. I could see their suffering, and all I could do was continue wearing a mask. I was trying to be positive and brave for them when inside I was dying. I never spoke to them about what happened to me or what was happening. We never consulted them or asked them how they were feeling. They were children; I had to protect them. This is the one thing I would come to regret in hindsight. All I knew, for their sake, was that I had to get better and do better, and if they trusted me, it would all go back to how it used to be.

I was just going through the motions of my physical rehab but wasn't getting anywhere. I can't remember what gave me the spark of hope to keep going; it had to be supernatural and possibly the small, consistent

falling short

actions I took each day in rehab that helped. I was not used to seeing or believing that small daily actions would mean that change was possible. I always thought that big actions meant a big impact.

As I look back at almost hitting rock bottom, a failed suicide attempt, and being depressed with my diagnoses and plight, I was more disappointed and betrayed by everyone around me who I believe had failed me. The specialists, experts, my husband, family, church, friends, my body, mind, heart, and even my God.

7
the search

AT THAT POINT IN MY LIFE, I became desperate. I wanted everything to go back to how it used to be, back to when I was doing amazing, or so I believed. I began searching for answers, and New Age spirituality crossed my path. I knew the only way for me to rise from the dead would require doing or learning something that I had never experienced before.

I was done with church religion. When everything was going well, it worked. But, it didn't help in a real-life crisis, perhaps temporarily, but not during my dark season. It failed me miserably.

I found New Age spirituality to be very holistic. Their approach appealed to me because it focused on the whole being; mind, body, soul, and spirit. A big part that I believed the conventional system of medicine and religion missed. Although trying to be multi-disciplinary, the allopathic system never addressed the spiritual, energetic or emotional parts of a person that needed healing.

Once you heal your injury physically, you are taught new strategies to live within the scope of your limited pain threshold and never to push beyond that. This was the new quality of life I had been given to accept, and I couldn't accept that. I felt I was taught coping strategies and defence mechanisms as a band-aid to keep me comfortable. What it did was make me into a victim. It kept me bound to a story of pity. It was my set limit; I wouldn't dare defy or go against the expert advice because they were the specialists, right? They know what's best, and I did trust them, but I couldn't deny what my intuition and the leading of the Spirit was saying to me. That there could also be another way to heal and not have to live like this for the rest of my life?

In the New Age, spirituality, health, and wellness are viewed as abundance, so I began with my food and gut health. We had been consuming an organic and vegetarian diet for years, so we knew that our gut health was vital. Even though we weren't able to afford to eat healthier at this time, I told Ken that if we were going to survive and in order for me to heal, we had to make sacrifices. Sometimes when I reflect, I'm amazed that we could afford to eat this way because Ken wasn't working, and we were living solely on welfare at the time. We had no debt, which helped. After paying our rent, food was the priority.

Ken made an effort to try and cook while I was going through occupational therapy. They were teaching me how to move differently. It wasn't easy, but it was helpful. We bought new equipment to help me sit on a chair at the table to help guide Ken in the kitchen. It felt like old times.

I then began looking into natural remedies for pain relief. I started learning about essential oils, homeopathy, comfrey, and plant medicine. I stopped taking all prescribed medications, which was a real life-changer for me at that time. I changed my outpatient provider care from mainstream to natural therapy, which included: osteopathy, chiropractor, weekly lymphatic drainage massages, Chinese medicine, and kinesiology. I learned how to keep our home toxic-free by removing chemicals and synthetics products and replacing them with plant-based, natural, organic products, and began my children on their healing journey.

Little by little, I could see the different areas of my life improving. Now It was time to address my spiritual health.

Up until this point, I had only viewed my life through one lens, the church. I believe that everything that had happened to me was to test my faith. I was beginning to think that there was more to it than that. I had never really questioned God in depth nor spoken to him conversationally. I had been taught that it was disrespectful, but I had a sudden urge to approach him that way. During the spiritual moment in that first night at the hospital, I had honestly believed that everything I had done up to that point was all for him. I spoke to him about my confusion around faith, and this opened up a new dialogue.

Exploring new age practices for spiritual healing helped me unravel my religious confusion. For so long, I had been in my head, not feeling or thinking, just blindly following. I began practicing yoga, meditation, breathing, and moving in ways my body never had. Through so much frozen tension that had been stored in my body, I was learning about how to free my mind and engage in new levels of self-mastery.

Self-mastery became my hook. It was about looking within and levelling up. The thought of going to another level in the way I was thinking, feeling, and moving was enticing. I had only ever looked up for my answers, but now, I was looking within. For me, this felt new. The thought that I had always had the answers and solutions within was a new concept.

At the same time, I explored science from a new age spirituality lens. I was looking at the new concepts and trends like neuroscience, neuroplasticity, neurolinguistic, and neuromotor physiology. I thrived on new knowledge and practices, new ways of being. I believed I was healing, and I especially believed the church was outdated. The church, to me, was out of touch with true spirituality and humanity. So, I continued to stretch and explore.

I explored concepts like manifestation, abundance, and energy healing. Energy healing was not a new concept to me. My sister and brother-in-law practiced New Age spirituality, and it was their way of life. They often spoke about it, but I never understood it. I thought it was woo-woo. But understanding it lit up a dormant superpower within me. I used my deep spiritual intuition unconsciously, but because of my church beliefs, I tried to stay away from engaging in it because it had been viewed as evil. I found so much life as I became connected with my heart, body, soul, and mind. I also found my soul tribe.

I came to realize that I was lonely. It was the kind of loneliness that longed for deeper connection and conversations. In that community, I found that. I saw people who had the same desires to go beyond the surface of our beings. I knew that it was what I needed. I needed permission to go deeper, inquire, lean in, and explore endless possibilities of being. The permission to explore was liberating.

I had locked myself away from doing anything wrong, living by the law perfectly, in the hopes of having God's pleasure and approval. It only led me to exactly where I was, rebellion against my faith, feeling disconnected, and doubting all that I had been taught growing up, in light of this new truth.

Throughout my entire life, I battled with following the religious road that I was expected to. I was born into my faith and was never given the choice of discovering God for myself. From the moment I was born, it was a concept indoctrinated into me. I had followed all the church rules and laws to a T, as handed down from the bible through the church.

On the road to learning a new way of life, I learned the art of ceremony and sacred circle rituals, scripting, embodiment, breathwork, affirmations, and reiki. But eventually, I began to see huge gaps in my community around me. There was a massive spirit of discontentment and self-attainment, always chasing something more; a never-ending emotional rollercoaster.

This search caused a lot of conflict in my heart and home. Ken wanted to be supportive, this was a part of my healing, but it went against his own beliefs. I was so quick to believe that it was what I needed and quickly convinced everyone that it was what I had been looking for my whole life. It wasn't Ken's journey. It was mine. But he chose to support me the best way he knew how. He'd voice his concerns every now and then and asked me questions about these new practices, but I felt I had to be in defence mode, justifying what I was doing.

His doubt put doubt into my mind and heart, which I perceived as him not being loving or supportive. I would often remind him how I always supported everything he did, and I only demanded the same respect back whether he agreed with it or not. It was my life, not his. I had my own thoughts and beliefs around what was becoming my new truth, and I wasn't asking him for permission.

I found myself attacking his church and their old fashioned beliefs. I would point out what I believed to be their errors, corrupt system, and fake believers who were all hoarding knowledge and not doing anything to change people's lives. The more I dived in, the more I was pulling away from God and my family. I was soaking in an experience I had never had in the church. There was a deep sense of belonging and acceptance. The rebel in me was welcomed, even praised. I was no longer the outcast who had her own thoughts, feelings, and ideas. I didn't have to prove anything to anybody. It was a levelled playing field. Everyone was there to cheer you on and see you live your best life. I was in a bubble of bliss, where the new truth had no flaws or human errors. I was delusional, not entirely in my right state of mind, although I thought I was. My emotions were sweeping me up.

One day, during a ceremony ritual at a retreat, I sensed strong evil spirits. It was something I had unfortunately experienced before. I knew from that moment that New Age Spirituality was not the way for me. It all seemed like love and light on the surface, but the deeper I went, underneath the veil, the deeper I saw that it was all quite empty.

Many amazing things and learnings came from this season of searching for healing in other places foreign to what I had always known. For those discoveries, I will always be grateful. They created a sense of empowerment that has stuck with me. This time in my life showed me that I had been asleep for years, but I was finally awake. I met so many people that I consider my soul family. Although we may have different beliefs, we are still the best of friends and continue to learn how to connect holistically. This season changed my life forever.

I began to pick up my conversations with God, right where we left off. The first strong impression he gave me was to return to the church, not because it was the right way. To this day, I still don't attend church. It was solely to share my story with others and share what I had seen, heard, felt, and experienced. I didn't get it at the time. And I'm glad I didn't wait to be told the why. I just followed my intuition of where his Spirit was leading me.

8
denying myself

I WAS APPROACHING THE END of my rehabilitation program, which they call the "moving forward phase." It's all about what comes next for the outpatients and how to continue your recovery and maintain your care plan once your rehabilitation program has finished. One of the plan's recommendations was to try to do something that I had never done before my accident.

I was terrified. *Did this mean I couldn't be a stay at home mum anymore?* I'd have to look for a job with no qualifications, skills, or credentials. *Would I go back to school and study? Where would I begin?*

That same day, I spoke to a dear friend who was checking in to see how I was doing. She was an entrepreneur and had been for a while now. I was intrigued by how she lived her life. I told her what had happened at rehab that day, and she said to me about how easy it was to start your own online business. Well, that conversation took me down a rabbit hole of possibilities. Starting my own business became my new obsession.

I announced to Ken that I was going to start my own business and go back to university. Again, his level of reservation was hard to hide as he tried to be supportive. He felt like he had just got me back to only lose me down another rabbit hole. As always, he bit his tongue and supported me as best he could. I have never doubted his faith or belief in me. He is my biggest cheerleader; I believe for him, it has always been a matter of right and wrong. When we had both been living life through a religious lens, our life was based on what was right and what was wrong.

My first step was filling out the university application for matured education to study biomedical science. Then, I sat down to create a plan of what I needed to do to start my own business. Everything fell into place. I was accepted into university for online classes and signed up for my first business course. I set up my social media and was ready to rock n'roll.

denying myself

I didn't know that this season I was about to embark on would thrust me into an intense season of personal development—just when I thought I couldn't go any deeper, well, there were still more levels of uncovering to experience. This season would challenge me deeper in my marriage relationship, my relationship with my children, and my relationship with myself. I will share a few intense struggles I experienced during this time that came in the form of misalignment, inauthenticity, and where I had been hiding in the darkness.

I looked at what I had all my skills, talents, gifts, experiences, learnings, and created two businesses out of that. My greatest skills being storytelling and my personal experience. I brought storytelling, my life experience, and all the modalities I had been studying and learning in my healing season altogether, to support and serve others. Let Light In and Nurosteps were born.

Nurosteps was focused on helping parents and families whose children had difficulties with learning and behavioural development. I utilized my awareness around alternative options to provide support for their child's healing and to support families with many solutions as each child is unique. I did one to one consulting, eventually specialising in parent workshops and professional development training for teachers and allied health professionals.

Let Light In grew to be an online storytelling platform. It started out as a space to encourage teenagers to discover, design, and deliver their personal stories. My first program was 3D storytelling and my vision was to go into schools and run story workshops. Very quickly though, it changed and became a storytelling platform for millennial women. It changed many times before it took off, but it never lost the foundation or vision; to encourage others to share their story with the world.

Launching into the online world, spiraled me into an unhealthy relationship with personal development. It triggered anxiety in me. My performative perfectionism should have thrived here, but it was a whole new playing field. I was lost in it and didn't have much guidance or lead, so it only felt natural to then level up by reaching out to the "current experts" in the space and learn from them.

As I explored different business ideas, I knew that storytelling was my thing. Storytelling is a popular marketing tool but not something people would think to start a business around. There was no blueprint for me to follow, which was scary to think about creating my own.

I hired several business coaches because I was telling myself the same story, I didn't know anything. So I had to be told what and how things needed to be done.

denying myself

I paid for branding before I even knew what my business was. This resulted in my branding changing five times, along with my website and message changing a hundred times more. I invested thousands and thousands of dollars into masterminds, online courses, coaches, and retreats. It just didn't stop. I thought it would end once I received the information and knowledge I needed but it was never enough. There was always the next best and something that I still didn't know. It was insane.

I lost count of how many free offers I signed up for. I was gleaning for the right resource that I thought would change my life and elevate my business. I was constantly focused on the amount of money I wasn't making, the number of followers I had, and how many likes I was getting. It was an addictive gig, obsessing over the analytics.

I tried everything, various tips, and strategies, even trying to be more like someone else, which felt super awkward. None lasted very long, or weren't the right fit for how I wanted my business to look, be and feel like.

It was exhausting! But I wasn't giving up and I kept fighting. I loved what I did, the work was not the problem, it was the systems and business logistics. I wanted this to work, to have some kind of success, even if it killed me. I wanted to share my heart and love with the world. I wanted to show people how far I had come in my journey after all that had happened to me. Failing was not an option. It would be another hit of humiliation, my vulnerable heart couldn't take.

Sifting out the voices and trying to ground myself was almost impossible in a noisy marketplace. It was hard not to compare, admire, copy or become paralysed by all the information and the influencers in the online world.

I wasn't able to keep up with my studies. I passed the first two years, but then had to put that on pause so that I could focus on my business, hustling hard to make it work, I felt as if everyone was watching me closely, every action, word, caption written, story and post. The judgment I felt from others, I had never really encountered before. The level of scrutiny, even though you're behind a screen, the pressure to show up and be your authentic self on the daily created legit pains!

After a few years of pouring my energy into the online space, I got sick with pneumonia. Oh, and I was pregnant, with baby number eight. I'll be honest, I wasn't thrilled. I was so focused on making my businesses successful, but I was extremely sick. I had been hospitalized for a total of eight times due to my pregnancy and other illnesses. Getting sick has always been an indicator for me to check-in with myself and reflect.

denying myself

That's exactly what I needed to do. I ended up having an emergency c-section.

Uriah Jordan came into the world in November 2018. It was a magical experience. His name means God is my light. As I kissed him for the first time, I prayed over him. I prayed that his light would always shine in the darkness and be a light to others around him.

Giving birth is the most powerful way to rebirth yourself. I could feel new life breathing into me; my body and business. It was a pivotal moment. But that moment was short-lived. I received news that I had to appear in court days later. I ended up losing my drivers license for a whole year, not because of my driving or any traffic infringements, it was an error and I couldn't prove otherwise. I had workshops to run, I had five new contracts to work in new schools and a newborn.

This made things rather tricky and challenging. I had no one to drive me and no spare driver, I had no way or means of getting support. I only saw one way and that meant sacrificing what I wanted to do. I sacrificed my work and money. I did work with Ken to still run my workshop, but everything else, I had chosen to put on pause and focus on my newborn, my home, and my family as the priority for the year.

During that year, I had a constant battle between my heart and my head. What I knew needed my attention in my home versus what I wanted to do. There had never been such an intense swing of having to choose between myself and my family before. It didn't help that I didn't have a license and broke my foot but, I never had to choose between being a full-time stay at home mum versus being a working mum even with an online business. This struggle kept tugging on my heart. I believed that I couldn't do both, it had to be one or the other. I always had that black and white thinking; all or nothing. It was old school thinking.

The old school thinking teaches us that only men work and provide for the home. Women stay at home and are responsible for her husband, children, and church. I do love this way, but it was no longer serving my desires. Holding onto this way of life was me not acknowledging my growth; I had changed.

Once upon a time, I remember judging mother's who were in the workforce, who chose to pursue their ambitions and careers over their families. According to my standards, they weren't able to do it all and do it well. But it was time for me to eat my own humble pie.

Why couldn't I do it all? Why couldn't I have both? Why did it have to be one or the other?

How could I make it work where I could live out my purpose as well as be there for my family? How were so many

denying myself

women doing it? What was the truth around this martyring belief that I had to sacrifice myself for some greater good?

What an illusion and distorted belief that this was just the way it was. Even if I could do it all, something will always give way somehow, most likely my health and joy. There would always be more sacrifices to make along the way and I think it would eventually only make me resentful towards myself, my business, and my family.

Having the perfect work, life, home balance; is not real. It was time for me to let this belief go. The more I tried to resist the more objections I had. Whilst I am a ninja at homemaking, not even I could give one hundred percent all of the time, to everything.

Flexibility requires meeting the needs in the present moment. It gives us space to not feel we always have to be in control. It allows us to be imperfect and eventually live empowered.

The struggle between my head and heart came down to knowing what I believe in and working on changing those beliefs that didn't serve me. I stopped struggling with having to choose one or the other; family or dreams.

There became less tension at home but I still had to deal with my online business. To be honest, I love social media. I love seeing, cheering for, and encouraging others. It fuelled my heart. But, every time it came to me being in front of the camera, I cringed at my face, body, and the words that came out of my mouth. It didn't matter if it was a video or photo. I tried to challenge myself, to push myself outside of my comfort zone but it was excruciating. *Why is this so hard? Why do I care so much about what people think? Why do I think so low of myself?*

I had constant narratives running through my head that told me I wasn't pretty, knowledgeable, or smart enough. I questioned who I was to be sharing my personal experiences. *Who was I, why would anyone want to listen to me?* The confidence I once had was gone. I felt like I had a muzzle over my mouth, stopping me from using my voice and I was constantly judging myself. All of this blocked me from reaching any kind of the success I was craving. Although I received positive feedback and encouragement in my business, it all felt like a lie. Deep down, I felt inauthentic and out of alignment, at some point surely, this kind of internal rollercoaster has to stop, right? I felt my heart was yearning for rest and I needed to retreat for a season.

True to my Jen style, I had to confront this head-on. *Why was I feeling this way?*

I don't think I will ever be able to do things without full effort, as much as I tried to take my time to address

denying myself

all that was happening in my heart and mind slowly or unpack it bit by bit, I just couldn't help myself and threw myself all in. You know what? That's ok! It may not be for everyone to always be full-blown, pedal to the metal. This isn't something that drains me, it's actually the opposite for me, it's motivation and I own it. In saying that I do have big spurts of rest in between that fuel the risks I need to take, this is my balance.

With a bit more kindness, I hired a support coach, so I didn't feel that I had to do this all on my own. I began to unpack the unhealthy relationship I had with myself around my identity and who I really am.

Going through everything I had been through and trying to figure out how to heal along the way, I realised how much I didn't know or recognise who I was anymore. I had lost myself along the way. It's easy for this to happen when you're stuck in your story and everything that has happened to you. I didn't know how to live outside of my story or circumstances. It is one thing to be resilient, come through as a survivor, yet still live in a survivor's mindset. I'm still in healing mode.

It took me starting a business and coming into the light to unveil this truth to me: showing up publicly requires authenticity, vulnerability, and another level of courage that I had been hiding behind, for so long. I had come through some dark times, yes the big events were public, but dealing with it and processing my emotions, thoughts, and feelings, all of that was done in the shadows. Being out in the open, even though it's not in person, allowed me to fast track my journey and be laser-focused.

I stopped worrying about my business, and focused on myself but not from a healing perspective. The laser-focused perspective of being a Daughter of God, woman, wife, mother, sister, friend, and server to others. And in that order too.

I had been raised in a religion and a culture, where it was all about what not to do. Don't do this, don't do that. What I went through, allowed me to see, very clearly, what no longer served me and what I no longer valued. This purge was based on untwisting old beliefs and shedding my old skin, which was only one part of my healing and unlearning. What I hadn't learned yet was where and how I was going to move forward from there and why I continued to be stuck in my story.

Is this all there is?

Denying my new identity, my growth, and the truth that I was a completely different woman, is what was stifling my full healing, business, and self-development. It was liberating to let all of that go! The judgment I felt from everyone was my own. I was afraid of losing friendships, respect, and trust, but finding out who

denying myself

I am, my voice, truth and purpose, is worth all those losses to gain peace of mind, and heart. It's always been there, in me, buried under the many layers that I placed on myself.

9

fought

THE LAST 40 YEARS of my life have been one continuous fight. From the moment I entered this world to today I have fought and am still fighting. I've been fighting to stay alive, fighting for what I believe in, and fighting to figure out who I am. From a young age, I believed that if I wanted something, I had to do it on my own.

I've fought for my health.
I've fought for acceptance.
I've fought to prove myself.
I've fought for permission.
I've fought for my life; to stay alive.

I've fought for my reputation.
I've fought for my family; my husband and children.
I've fought for strangers.
I've fought to be seen.
I've fought to be heard.
I've fought for my faith.
I've fought for my voice.
I've fought for my identity.
I've fought for validation.
I've fought for my truth.
I've fought for work.
I've fought for my heart.
I've fought for freedom.
I've fought for my authenticity.

I took pride in seeing myself as a fighter. But when you are fighting from a place of survival, you eventually become worn down. You are left with no sense of reasoning or critical thinking and end up making poor decisions. You end up losing the fight within yourself. Your heart and mind become preoccupied with what I call toxic tenants. These are the kind of tenants who don't pay rent, they trash the place, make unrealistic demands, and then leave the place in one big mess. This was my mind. It became a battlefield. All I can do, or we can do, is cope the best we know-how. Sometimes, that

fought

affects our physical, emotional, mental, or spiritual well being. Sometimes, we give into unrealistic demands and expectations of false peace and safety.

Another fight is the fight for survival. Striving to know all answers, to do, or have the next best thing. Your mind never quits. It races around in circles with no rest. It's a constant feeling of pushing, manipulation, strategizing, and wanting control of everything.

Then we have the victim mentality fight. We tell ourselves we're broken and we cannot be fixed. We're always searching for healing. Along my journey, I found many band-aid fixes that provided valuable lessons when I needed them. But nothing substantial. Once I wasn't satisfied, it was a search for the next best thing.

There was a constant cycle of fighting. Encountering tragic events and holding distorted beliefs only exacerbates that cycle and you feel stuck.

My desire to live and love from an authentic place of alignment seemed like a dream I had no idea where to begin, I felt like I exhausted all options. But I was longing for freedom from this vicious cycle.

How does one reprogram their way of being and doing?

By slowing down. Do the exact opposite of what you're used to doing. This is exactly what I had to do for myself. This opened the door for new discoveries that made a profound impact on where I am today in my life;

they are powerful concepts that will break any patterns or conditions.

Acceptance with Joy

What happened to me was for me and that is what accepting with joy looks like. This helped me break the victim mentality I was clinging to. I viewed everything as a tragedy and being the victim was justified because of it. The tragedies were unfair and unjust but, in life, some things are out of our control; no matter how hard we fight to control them. Joy brought a deepened level of trust in myself and others around me, and a deeper level of empathy towards others. It helped me see beyond the present circumstances or unhelpful beliefs I was holding onto when it came to testing my faith. For so long I was fighting a fight of faith. I wanted to show the world how well I was fighting, how quickly I could recover, and that I was filled with positivity at all times. It was a show for the other believers around me and had nothing to do with my relationship with God. Acceptance with joy is about trust. In no way does it mean that you need to be a robot and not feel grief, anger, or doubt. Acceptance with joy is accepting that you are human but you trust in God and everything happening; even when it feels unfair. Sometimes we need a reminder to come back to trust because it's not easy to remain in this space at all times. I reclaimed my power, even though my trust was not in myself, but in God.

Personal Responsibility

What did I do wrong? I'm the victim! Taking responsibility was a foreign concept to me. It seems strange that when things happen to us that are out of our control, that we have some kind of responsibility. The thing is, we always have a choice in how we respond to life events. My level of respond-ability was immature. Living from a place of survival meant my responses were reactive because I was trying to cope and keep myself safe from pain and fear. So I had to take back responsibility for my choices in each moment. For example, I had to take ownership that this didn't only happen to me, but also Ken and our children; it was eye-opening. I took responsibility for the way I had placed little value on their lives and needed to apologise for that. I took responsibility for the emotions and feelings I harboured towards myself and others. Forgiveness being the antidote for painful resentment. I took responsibility for my actions, words, vows, and criticism, pulling away from blame, who wanted to be continuously justified for its poor behaviour. I took responsibility for believing lies and dispelling them with truths. I took responsibility for the stories I was telling myself and others and rewrote my narrative.

Taking personal responsibility reclaimed my power in a way that separated truth and error. I could now see objectively beyond moral concepts of what was right and wrong.

Breakdown the Strongholds

You can't change what you don't know. A stronghold in biblical terms is about something that has a hold over you in a negative way, figuratively speaking. In these seasons of my life that I have shared here, I realized that many spiritual things had a hold on my life that I needed to be set free from. There were intergenerational traumas; there were stories in the past and lies that were at the foundation of why I lived the way I did. There was a deep shame that I needed to deal with, distorted beliefs about myself and my faith that I needed to confront, this was inner work that needed to come to light because I was hiding.

fought

It wasn't easy, it was brutal. Brutal in the sense that I had to be completely honest with myself and call myself out for what the truth was. When you've been living at surface level for a very long time, and in my default cycle, this is not as easy as it may sound. This takes a willingness that your strongholds can be defeated. It started with believing.

I had already begun doing this work in my seasons of searching and unravelling. I had been identifying the strongholds that had power over me. You can't break down what you don't know exists. At this point in my life, after all that I had been through, I felt a strong pull to take up God's invitation to come and get to know him. Instead of going through the church, I let go of what I thought I knew prior and came back to his invitation with an open perspective and clean slate.

Journeying with God this time around has been completely different. I followed the Holy Spirit, who spoke through my heart. In this season of my life, I was being led to get to know him again in a more intimate way without barriers. I was guided to work with a mentor, who has a special gift for deliverance and inner healing. We had intense sessions, confessions, repentance, and full restoration with the Lord. My strongholds came tumbling down and my heart was redeemed.

Redemption, in this season, was taking back my power through my ultimate power source; Jesus. He rescued my misaligned heart from a toxic cycle and restored me to my true identity.

As this part of my story comes to an end, these cycles end with these stories coming into full view and leaving all of it behind. The journey to authenticity is so worth the fight. I redeemed my hidden heart at last!

> "To everything, there is a season, and a time to every purpose under the heaven: A time to be born, and a time to die; a time to plant, and a time to pluck up that which is planted; a time to kill, and a time to heal; a time to break down, and a time to build up; a time to weep, and a time to laugh; a time to mourn, and a time to dance; a time to cast away stones, and a time to gather stones together; a time to embrace, and a time to refrain from embracing; a time to get, and a time to lose; a time to keep, and a time to cast away; a time to rend, and a time to sew; a time to keep silence, and a time to speak; a time to love, and a time to hate; a time of war, and a time of peace."
>
> —**KING SOLOMON**

The journey continues...

acknowledgements

TO MY LORD AND MY BEST FRIEND JESUS, who is my all in all, thank you for never leaving me even when I rejected and walked away from you. Thank you for loving me unconditionally and gently wooing my heart back to know who you truly are! Eternally grateful!

To my soul mate, rock and life partner, Ken, I don't think I could ever have the right words to express how much I love you and the life we have created together. Thank you always for having patience, unconditional support and loving me so deeply, I feel it through every look, word, thought and touch! I adore you! Forever blessed.

To my special children who transformed my whole world and who are my greatest life teachers—Jireh, Ezreh, Zion, Rehnee, Reymah, Torah, Neareh and Uriah, thank you for enriching my life on the daily, you are my why, my adventure and firsthand experiences.

To my mum and dad, my biggest cheerleaders in life, thank you for showing me what faith, family, community and loving others are all about. Thank you for your support and always believing in me, no matter what! I love you both immensely.

To all my siblings—all 15 of you. Thank you all for the endless, treasured memories of belly laughs, good times, bad times, conspiracies, fun, having each other back, support and love. Big love always.

To my inner circle, my best friends, my sisters—Barbara, Yonita and Jordan. Without you three, life would be so boring! Thank you for always having my back, for taking care of all the details, for being the best soundboards, second mamas for our children, for loving and cheering me on always!

To all of my mentors, coaches, support team, I have encountered through my life journey to arrive where I'm at today, thank you for seeing in me who I forgot that I was and thank you for your guidance. I will forever be grateful.

To all my special friendships who are all extended family! We have been through all these storms together! Thank you for your prayers, love and support. A special mention to my fire sisters—Janna, Connie, Lise and Simone, you four prayer warriors, faith sisters, you have had a profound impact on my faith and heart—all heaven bound!

To all my awesome communities around the world—So much love for you all! I honour you for entrusting

acknowledgements

me with your stories and being with me on my own story journey.

To Ashley-Ann, my amazing publisher, thank you for making this dream a reality. Thank you for believing in my story before I believed it was worth writing myself and thank you for your patience to capture my conversational style, not easy to edit! Love ya girl! X

JEN WRIGHT comes from a line of Orators, chiefs, reformers, healers and warriors. She is a mother, storyteller, speaker and activist. Her journey has led her to create the Storyteller Tour and Bodyteller Tour.

She is passionate about sharing her faith in God, wellbeing, spending time with her family, building intentional communities, activating prophetic voices, standing for truth, freedom, justice and systemic reform.

You can follow her journey on Instagram @redeemher.heart, @jenwright_voice or her telegram channel—Voice in the wilderness.

www.ingramcontent.com/pod-product-compliance
Lightning Source LLC
Chambersburg PA
CBHW030307100526
44590CB00012B/555